THE HUDSON RIVER SCHOOL

Contents

INTRODUCTION

Go forth, under the open sky, and list to
Nature's teachings, while from all around –
Earth and her waters, and the depths of air –
Comes a still voice.

William Cullen Bryant, *Thanatopsis*, 1811

As risk-taking explorers of the early nineteenth century, the first American landscape painters struggled for acceptance in the European art world through their popular representations of the dramatic American wilderness. Responding to the ideals expressed by their companion and patron, William Cullen Bryant, they were determined to examine the world around them in great detail, in all seasons, and to present that world with reverence on canvas.

These artists climbed trees, paddled jungle streams, hiked exhausting miles, joined exploration parties and endured months of comfortless trail life – in order to record and interpret, in thousands of sketches, the beauty and mystery of the natural world. The resulting revolutionary paintings would one day find themselves grouped as the Hudson River School. Not all of these landscape painters documented Hudson River scenery, but they all painted in huge studios in New York City near the mouth of the Hudson between 1825 and 1875.

It was only at the end of its fifty-year lifespan that this first significant body of landscape work was given the title, Hudson River School. Some art historians have since preferred calling

it the First New York School or even the Native School, which included art forms other than landscape. Nevertheless, while the original title was not meant kindly, its descriptive value has endured.

In Europe at the time, Romanticism in art and literature was marked by an interest in nature and in themes eliciting the imagination and emotions in the Gothic taste – full of mystery, fantasy and the supernatural. European painters were preoccupied with the sublime representation of nature characteristic of the Romantic movement – "sublime" meaning a beauty that encompassed grandeur, solitude, darkness and terror. Storms and their aftermath, ruins, lightning-scorched trees – all were images utilized by European painters and early American landscape artists. The lyrical yet carefully structured landscapes of the French artist Claude Lorraine, as well as the wild and forbidding paintings of the Italian Salvator Rosa, served as models for American landscape artists and were purchased by eager American travelers as mementos from their European tours.

American tourists returned from Europe to find fashionable travel books that glorified and popularized the American landscape. *American Scenery*, printed in 1840 and illustrated by William Henry Bartlett, was the most celebrated publication of its type. It contained engravings primarily of the Catskill Mountains and the Hudson River region but also included the scene from the Connecticut River Valley made famous by Thomas Cole's painting *View from Mt. Holyoke (The Oxbow)*.

Promising young American artists, aspiring to the goals of the Romantic period, typically spent their formative years at the important art centers in Europe. After studying first at the London studio of American artist Benjamin West, they would then journey to the center of the mid-nineteenth-century art world, Rome, or to Dusseldorf, Germany. In Rome, students such as Worthington Whittredge and Thomas Cole became absorbed in the Romantic preoccupation with the rise and fall of empires and their ruins.

The paintings displayed at the popular Dusseldorf Gallery in New York City reflected the refined techniques of European art training that were so enticing to young artists like Albert Bierstadt, who studied in Dusseldorf before proceeding on to Rome.

Thomas Nast, "Difficult Travelling" **(above left)**, "In the Woods" **(above)** and "The Artist in the Mountains" **(left)**. Three woodcuts from "Sketches Among the Catskill Mountains," *Harper's Weekly* 10 (21 July 1866), pp.456-57.

Not only did the gallery offer popular genre paintings of everyday life, it included the newer forms of landscape painting from Europe that influenced the work of Bierstadt and other landscape artists.

Equally important to the climate that nurtured the American landscape movement was the Romantic spiritual view of nature that emphasized man's union with nature as constituting the highest morality; if man could be rid of all artifices that kept him from his natural state, he would be freed of evil and unhappiness. Prominent American writers of the period, such as Washington Irving, James Fenimore Cooper and William Cullen Bryant, all expounded on the virtues of the natural state as the highest state of being. Irving's "Rip Van Winkle," Cooper's *The Last of the Mohicans*, and Bryant's poems helped in shaping an audience ready to receive the same message on canvas. Artists like Washington Allston and Thomas Cole, in regarding their paintings as more than just "leaf pictures," echoed the sentiments of such morally uplifting themes in their landscapes.

In a nation still yearning for an artistic identity of its own, the years 1825 to 1875, defining the Hudson River School, were a period of powerful nationalism in a young America. The earliest, dramatic and uniquely American landscapes of Thomas Cole prompted immediate response from a people restless to discover and claim its own greatness. These sentiments reached their pinnacle in the monumental and inspirational canvases of Frederic Church's *Niagara* and Albert Bierstadt's *Yellowstone Falls*.

Portraiture and historical documentary painting had dom-

Top: William H. Bartlett, "Entrance to the Highlands near Anthony's Nose, Hudson River," pencil and watercolor. The engraving was first published in *American Scenery* (1840).

Above: Photograph of James Fenimore Cooper by Mathew Brady.

Above: Thomas Cole, *Landscape Scene from "The Last of the Mohicans,"* 1827, oil on canvas, 25×31 in. New York State Historical Association, Cooperstown, NY.

Above: Washington Allston, *Elijah in the Desert*, 1817, oil on canvas, 48¾×72½ in. Courtesy, Museum of Fine Arts, Boston. Gift of Mrs. Samuel Hooper and Miss Alice Hooper.

inated American artistic expression until the spotlight turned to Thomas Cole, and suddenly an art form appeared that perfectly responded to the needs of a growing nation. Landscapes enlightened viewers with the purity of the natural ideal and glorified the often remote and even terrifying grandeur of topographical wonders. Moreover, in transcending the stately art forms of portraiture and historical tributes – present only in certain private homes and grand public institutions – these landscapes offered a universal, more democratic artistic expression to be exhibited in any parlor and admired by any viewer.

There was a public sense of ownership of these landscape paintings by the American people. Americans embraced this artwork, as reflected by their impressive attendance at landscape exhibitions and by their many purchases of such work. During this fifty-year period, landscape painters were able to make a respectable living solely through their art. The destitute twenty-four-year-old Thomas Cole, living in an unheated attic as a student, found himself besieged by commissions as soon as he began to produce American scenery based on his abundant and detailed wilderness sketches. Frederic Church and Albert Bierstadt garnered enormous fortunes in a decade, with their paintings commanding as much as $25,000 a piece, sums considered phenomenal even today. Not since that time has a body of original artwork received such thorough acceptance by the American people.

Above: Thomas Doughty, *View from Stacey Hill,* 1830.

THE OASIS IN US

Only a scattering of early American painters had considered landscape worthy of their attention, but their pioneering efforts were only occasionally appreciated and were never featured as serious art. Washington Allston was the most significant portrayer of the American landscape in the early 1800s. He dramatized myths and religious themes within his romantic landscapes. Well-suited to the Gothic fashion of the day, Allston's work was imaginative and passionate, straddling the two worlds of heroic moral tales and the budding universe of pure landscape.

It was Thomas Doughty, however, who provided the most important groundwork for public acceptance of American landscape paintings as valuable and significant. He was a self-taught painter from Philadelphia who abandoned his leather trade for painting, successfully receiving commissions to paint views of the estates of the wealthy. His works were exhibited at The Pennsylvania Academy of the Fine Arts, where they were much admired by the young Thomas Cole in 1823. As the first American artist to make his living by painting exclusively American landscapes, Doughty brought commitment and vision to his canvases.

9

work has become legendary. Trumbull was a painter of grand historic scenes in honor of the American Revolution, in which he was a commander. He became the president of the only arts institution in the new republic, the American Academy of Fine Arts in New York, which championed classical European art forms. Once when Trumbull passed by a New York frame shop window display in 1825, the famous painter spotted several striking landscapes of the Catskill Mountains. Not only did he inquire eagerly of this artist, Thomas Cole, who highlighted the American wilderness, he purchased one of the paintings on display. Trumbull soon returned to the shop with artist Asher Durand and art critic William Dunlap, each of whom bought the remaining two paintings; with these purchases, the name of Thomas Cole came into public focus.

Cole's move to New York and display of his Hudson River Valley landscapes coincided with the pageantry of the opening of the Erie Canal. As a symbol of the nation's post-War of 1812 prosperity and optimism, the canal opened up lands to the west for economic development. Providing a safe and scenic highway, the canal allowed travelers to view firsthand the wonders of nature that so captivated Thomas Cole. As people gravitated toward the unspoiled beauty of new territory, they were also drawn to Cole's detailed, mysterious landscapes.

In 1825 when the Erie Canal opened, there were no states in existence beyond the Mississippi River and no tamed pastoral landscape beyond the Hudson River. All territory beyond the coastal settlements was viewed with fear and mystery, and only the most venturesome made their way over rough roads barely cut through dense forests and forbidding mountains. The "wilderness" also implied the spiritual state of danger and temptation, as in the biblical wanderings of the Jews in the wilderness.

Thus, the promotion of tourist travel to remote lodges, like the Catskill Mountain House, for viewing scenic grandeur was

Deeply affected by James Fenimore Cooper's novels, portraying the power and purity of the natural state, Doughty introduced into his works the characteristics of the Hudson River School that made the "new" landscapes unique – devotion to detail and accuracy, idealization of setting and mood, and compositions of an orderly structure as exemplified in the landscapes of the Dusseldorf School. The message was clear: nature is noble, and a refuge, both spiritual and physical.

The story of John Trumbull's discovery of Thomas Cole's

Above: Thomas Cummings, *Thomas Cole*, oil on canvas, 36¼ × 29¼ in. Collection of the Albany Institute of History and Art. Bequest of Mrs. Florence Cole Vincent.

Right: John Trumbull, *The Death of General Warren at the Battle of Bunker Hill*, 1786, oil on canvas, 25 × 34 in. Yale University Art Gallery, New Haven, CT.

often given in "pilgrimage" language. Journeys into the White Mountains of New Hampshire and the Catskills of New York were considered spiritual experiences, bringing one closer to God. The spectacular sunrises from the Catskill Mountain House were compared to creation; the morning mists, such as those over the Connecticut River "Oxbow" below Prospect House on Mount Holyoke, were compared to the chaos out of which God created nature; the mist would lift, suddenly exposing the grandeur below.

In 1831, like all aspiring artists in America, Thomas Cole determined to travel in Europe to immerse himself in the great art centers of the world. Those who had come to treasure Cole's American artistic spirit cautioned him against the entrapment of the European establishment. Most famous in his admonition was William Cullen Bryant in his poem, "To Cole, the Painter, Departing for Europe":

> Fair scenes shall greet thee where thou goest – fair
> But different – everywhere the trace of men, . . .
> Gaze on them, till the tears shall dim thy sight,
> But keep that earlier, wilder image bright.

After experiencing the sense of drama and downfall visible in the great ruins of Rome, Thomas Cole was increasingly drawn to the Romantic visions of man's destiny in nature. Based upon the images and moral lessons Cole had gathered in Italy, his two ambitious series of paintings, *The Course of Empire* and *The Voyage of Life* were of personal importance to him. In these series, Cole retained the Romantic vision of Washington Allston, while his other popular nature paintings provided reliable income and became the foundation for the flowering American landscape art that grew up around him in New York.

The economic expansion of mid-nineteenth-century America provided artists with wealthy collectors who exhibited the impressive landscapes in their huge new parlors. An extraordinary patron of the new landscape art, Luman Reed made his fortune by 1832 through the shipping of produce via the Erie Canal. Reed commissioned Thomas Cole to paint his great five-canvas vision of *The Course of Empire*. Sadly for the entire art community, Luman Reed died in 1836, and *The Course of Empire*, as well as the rest of Reed's collection, was

Above: Thomas Cole, pencil sketch for *The Oxbow*, c. 1833. © The Detroit Institute of Arts, 8⅞ × 13¾ in. Founders Society Purchase, William H. Murphy Fund (39.566.67).

Left: Asher B. Durand, *Portrait of Luman Reed*, c. 1830s. Courtesy of The New-York Historical Society, New York, NY.

finally donated to the New York State Historical Society, where it resides today.

In this series of paintings, Cole exulted in the opportunity to bring one of his great hopes to fruition – to illustrate the progression of a culture from "savagery" to high civilization and back to the natural landscape. For Cole, nature was always the perfect spiritual state and "progress" must be tempered by careful and gradual development of a nation's resources; subduing the wilderness must not mean rampant destruction. In the end, Cole was convinced that nature would ultimately prevail in spite of man's efforts at permanent alteration.

Thomas Cole's "Essay on American Scenery," delivered as a lecture in 1835, perfectly combined the Romantic idealism of his time with a response to the headlong economic development that pushed the nation westward. The listeners were urged to nurture "the oasis in us" as a retreat from the world of "practical economy, or progress and fashion." Cole exhorted:

> The pleasures of the imagination, among which the love of scenery holds a conspicuous place, will alone temper the harshness of such a state; and, like the atmosphere that softens the most rugged forms of the landscape, cast a veil of tender beauty over the asperities of life.

In 1836 *The Course of Empire* was exhibited at the National Academy of Design as a special attraction. While it was glowingly praised by William Cullen Bryant and James Fenimore Cooper, the series was never a popular success with viewers or

critics. This audience continued to resist the moralizing efforts of painters like Cole and waited eagerly for authentic American landscape images. By 1839, it was the pure landscape that began to fix American art in the minds of the European art world. As expressed by a European critic of the day concerning the state of American art, "The American school of landscape is decidedly and peculiarly original; fresh, bold, brilliant and grand." Nevertheless, Cole continued to paint pictures with "moral value" upon which he felt his reputation truly stood.

In 1839, Cole was commissioned to paint *The Voyage of Life* series for Samuel Ward. These paintings were originally to hang in Ward's meditation room, a type of private chapel in his home. However, as with the "Empire" paintings, once again Cole's patron died before this important series of four paintings was finished. At the time, *The Voyage of Life* was also never well received by the viewing public, and only recently has the series been given the prominence in his body of work that Cole had intended.

After moving to his wonderful home in upstate New York, with its spectacular view of the Hudson River, Thomas Cole continued to paint the many treasured "wilderness" scenes sought by his supporters and to plan pieces for the spiritual instruction of his viewers. When Cole suddenly died of pneumonia in 1847, at the age of only 48, the American art world was stunned by the loss of its trailblazing painter of the American wilderness.

THROUGH THE TRANSPARENT ABYSS

. . . pictures which carried the eye over scenes of wild grandeur particular to our country, over our aerial mountain tops with their mighty growth of forest never touched by the ax, along the banks of streams never deformed by culture, and into the depth of skies bright with the hues of our own climate, skies such as few but Cole could ever paint, and through the transparent abyss of which you might send an arrow out of sight.

William Cullen Bryant

By the 1840s, the landscape movement had settled into an energetic pattern of growth. With the aid of countless sketches drawn during sojourns amidst nature, the successors of Thomas Cole spent months in their New York studios creating pictures of undomesticated landscapes, which bore no relationship to the ordered pastoral scenes of Europe. These artists succeeded in forming a new art association, the National Academy of Design, in reaction to the traditional American Academy of Fine Arts. Led by John Trumbull, the American Academy was devoted to European-style paintings and sculpture–portraits, grand historical chronicles on canvas, and reproductions of classical masterpieces. Determined to have a different focus from the American Academy, four months after its founding, the National Academy presented its first exhibit of 170 works, most of them landscapes, by living American artists.

Prior to the founding of the National Academy in 1826, there were no galleries or museums focusing on American artwork and no schools in America for art training. The very existence of the National Academy provided valuable encouragement to emerging artists, and its exhibits each year were significant events for each contributor. With famous artists such as Samuel F. B. Morse and Asher Durand guiding it, the National Academy helped in securing the reputations and fortunes of the significant landscape painters. Even in the design of its new building built in 1865, the National Academy glorified nature through its architectural ornament, reflecting the dominant emphasis of its artist members.

By the 1850s, nearly all of the Hudson River School artists maintained large studios in a single building in New York City. Working in their 15 West Tenth Street building, these painters entertained merchants, writers, doctors, professors – all eager to share in the devotion to the wilderness. The studios became a humming male social center whenever the artists were not sketching on location. It was a remarkably cooperative atmosphere, built on good fellowship and delight in each other and their wonderful subject matter. The fortunate circumstances of being able to provide a nationalistic art form to an eager audience was a joy to these artists, who prospered financially as well. The emergence of commercial art dealers handled the growing art trade.

Opposite above: Thomas Cole, *The Savage State*, first of *The Course of Empire* series, 1836, oil on canvas, 39¼ × 63¼ in.

Opposite below: Thomas Cole, *The Consummation of Empire*, third of *The Course of Empire* series, 1836, oil on canvas, 51¼ × 76 in.

Right: Thomas Cole, *Desolation*, fifth of *The Course of Empire* series, 1836, oil on canvas, 39¼ × 63¼ in.

All courtesy of The New-York Historical Society, New York, NY.

Left: "New York National Academy of Design – At the Head of the Staircase," engraving. *Harper's Weekly* 14 (14 May 1870), p. 316. National Academy of Design, New York, NY.

Middle: Photo of the National Academy of Design building, c. 1860s.

Bottom: Woodcut of the gallery of the Art Union by S. Wallin. *American Art Union Bulletin* III (1849), p.6.

Opposite: Asher B. Durand, c. 1869, *carte de visite* from Mrs. Vincent Coyler's album. Photograph by American Phototype Company, New York City. The Metropolitan Museum of Art, David Hunter McAlpin Fund, 1952 (52.605).

New writers joined in praise of the landscape movement; Henry W. Longfellow, Nathaniel Hawthorne, Ralph Waldo Emerson and Henry David Thoreau replaced Irving, Cooper and Bryant as the literary counterparts of the Hudson River painters. The philosophy of transcendentalism in New England, as expressed in the writings of Emerson, Thoreau and others, became a supportive current of Romanticism. These writers believed that an individual's knowledge and experience could go beyond the self and the visible world to gain a closer understanding of God. In view of landscape painting, this literature focused specifically on the divinity in nature, encouraging Americans to experience the moral benefits of con-

templating their unspoiled surroundings as a visible manifestation of the invisible divinity. A landscape painting in one's home served as a reminder and an inspiration of God and his creation.

In 1839, a revolutionary marketing plan appeared in New York City called the "art union." Originally a European phenomenon, the American Art Union was in actuality a giant raffle designed to promote American art. By offering individuals a $5 ticket to win one of hundreds of artworks in any single year – with all purchasers receiving large engravings – the Art Union watched the populace become caught up in the extravaganza. Art Union managers purchased works from artists, anticipating that the large volume of tickets sold would still provide them a profit after the raffle. The Art Union's most impressive offer was made in 1848 with the raffle of Thomas Cole's original four-canvas masterpiece, *The Voyage of Life*; that year Art Union membership nearly doubled. Most of the thousands of paintings raffled off each year were in the Romantic realist style, both landscape and genre.

The Art Union eventually collapsed as a victim of its own excess. Its managers sought control of the art market and quarreled with the National Academy; the Union padded its offerings with cheaper, lower quality paintings, along with the finest works; and finally, the Union jeopardized its role in art promotion by affiliating itself with an abolitionist newspaper. Subsequently, an opposition newspaper took the Art Union to court, and the 1852 decision declared the Art Union dissolved as an illegal lottery. Unorthodox as it was, the Art Union had mobilized Americans of all economic and social strata behind the popular art of the day, and even though its demise was a loss to many young artists, what remained was a legacy of enthusiasm and patronage for art.

Asher Durand – patron, companion and successor to Thomas Cole – emerged in the 1850s as the dominant figure in the New York City art world. In 1855, the art journal *The Crayon* published Durand's "Letters on Landscape Painting." The important essays defined all the concepts embodied in the Hudson River School; nature was "fraught with high and holy meaning," and to alter it was to offend the Divine Spirit that created it. It was also clear that to Durand, America offered the purest form of nature.

Originally an engraver, Durand went on to become an acclaimed portrait artist. Subsequently, his contact with Thomas Cole transformed Durand into a painter of nature. Accompanying Cole on trips into the "wilderness," he began to paint directly from nature; the resulting closeup oil sketches of wood scenes are considered some of his finest work today. Whereas his larger, more formal and detailed works emphasized accuracy and faithfulness to each scene, his on-location oil sketches were less precise and more spontaneous. It is fitting that perhaps the most emblematic painting of the Hudson River School, *Kindred Spirits* – showing Thomas Cole and William Cullen Bryant in a classic Hudson River landscape – was created by the committed Durand, who for many years led

the way for the other Hudson River painters.

Considered essential to their artistic development, the careers of most young landscape painters during the 1850s included studies in Europe. Well before their fame was established in America, Worthington Whittredge, Sanford Gifford, and Albert Bierstadt spent a winter in Rome together. However, when news reached Rome that Frederic Church was receiving remarkable prices for his exotic landscapes back in New York, Whittredge returned to America as fast as possible to share in the success. In addition to leaving his leisurely life in Rome, Whittredge ceased producing European landscapes to be marketed in his hometown of Cincinnati; instead, he painted American landscapes in the Tenth Street studio building in New York City. Once established, he traveled to the American West to paint, along with Sanford Gifford and John Kensett. A major figure in the New York City art world, Whittredge eventually became president of the National Academy in the 1870s.

Sanford Gifford was another artist drawn to the paintings of Thomas Cole. Gifford's paintings of the Catskills reflect his many sketching trips to that region. He traveled extensively with Albert Bierstadt, and upon his return from Europe, Gifford became an active member of the Tenth Street studio building. His painting was interrupted by his enlistment during the Civil War, but after the war, he toured the Middle East and the American West, always interested in new, intriguing subject matter for his paintings.

John Kensett was also active during the Civil War, raising money for charity. His generosity and compassion made him one of the most beloved of the Hudson River painters. He led the fundraising effort in 1863 to erect the first National Academy building and was a founding member of the Metropolitan Museum of Art in 1870.

Kensett, and other landscape artists such as Jasper Cropsey, enjoyed painting the mountain regions of New York and New England, in particular, the Catskills. Whereas Cropsey's large canvas, *Autumn on the Hudson River*, secured his reputation as a premier painter of detailed autumn landscapes, Kensett's paintings were more preoccupied with light and its effects than with the detailed accuracy of a scene. Kensett, Gifford, and John Casilear all painted in what is now called the Luminist manner. Casilear studied under Asher Durand and became a friend and painting companion of both Kensett and Durand.

Until recently, the names of many of these respected Hudson River painters have been obscure. Kensett, Whittredge, Cropsey, Gifford, and others, all experienced substantial success as members of the National Academy and as contributors to the Art Union. Yet by 1900, with the decline in popularity and near disappearance of the Hudson River School's work, these artists were buried in art history. Their return to exhibitions highlighting the Hudson River School of painters, has enriched our understanding of that period in American art.

Right: John Kensett in his New York City studio, c. 1864. Photographs of Artists, Collection I, Archives of American Art, Smithsonian Institution.

Left: Jasper F. Cropsey, *Starrucca Vale*, October 15th, 1853, pencil and lightwash, touched with white on pale buff paper, $11\frac{13}{16} \times 18\frac{1}{2}$ in. Courtesy, Museum of Fine Arts, Boston, M. and M. Karolik Collection of American Watercolors and Drawings, 1800-1875 (52.1594).

Above: Frederic Church, *The Icebergs*, 1861,
oil on canvas, 64½ × 112⅜ in.
Dallas Museum of Art, anonymous gift (1979.28).

FROM SPECTACLE TO OBLIVION

In 1825, when Thomas Cole sold his first paintings, there were few American artists exploring the landscape form beyond that of folk representations. Certainly the earliest landscapes were not exhibited in any serious manner. Less than forty years later the great Metropolitan Fair in New York City – a three week exhibition held in 1864 – featured six hundred paintings, one-half of which were devoted to American landscape painting. Chaired by John Kensett, the fair was an impressive success.

As the Civil War brought devastation and despair to the nation, it simultaneously brought huge fortunes to northeastern businessmen. As the purchase of paintings for unprecedented sums became the fashion, landscape painters found themselves flourishing in a market waiting for every finished painting.

Some of the paintings on display at the 1864 Metropolitan Fair were donations toward the Union war effort, and many of the major artists of the day depicted the war years in their works, either specifically or symbolically. While some camp and battle scenes were documented in photographs, pencil and paint, Frederic Church's spectacular interpretation of a volcanic eruption in Ecuador, *Cotopaxi*, was viewed by many as an embodiment of the violent and fiery upheaval of the American conflict. Its very size, four feet by seven feet, reflected the magnitude of the searing years of the war.

Church and Albert Bierstadt were the greatest financial beneficiaries as the climate of wealth coincided with public presentations of some of their most dramatic paintings. While Church painted the splendors of his mountain journeys through Ecuador, Bierstadt depicted majestic scenery during his own excursion of discovery to California with the Landers expedition – an experience as full of danger, daring and drama as in any Gothic novel. After his return to New York City, which was flourishing in postwar prosperity, eager audiences at the Metropolitan Fair were ready to receive Bierstadt's work as their first introduction to the Far West. His painting *Rocky Mountains – Landers Peak* placed Bierstadt overnight "in the first rank of American genius," and the Romantic landscape movement reached its zenith.

The landscape perspective had expanded, encompassing distant exotic lands and newly discovered natural wonders in the American West. In addition, the original themes upon which landscape painting was founded, now moved away from the goal of inspiration and identification with the divine, toward effects "to astound but not elevate." Frederic Church's works embody many of the aspirations of his teacher, Thomas Cole – reflecting God in nature, using nature's grandeur to inspire, and carefully documenting nature's details. Albert Bierstadt, however, was accused of painting only to please and amaze his audience. Nevertheless, both men were extremely productive and became prosperous in a short time, reaping grand fees for their grand paintings.

In 1867, a great number of Hudson River School paintings were sent to the Paris Universal Exposition, at which both Church's *Niagara* and Bierstadt's *Rocky Mountains – Landers Peak* won awards. Finally, American painters were accepted on

Above: Albert Bierstadt, c. 1870.

Right: Albert Bierstadt, *Platte River, Nebraska*, 1863, oil on canvas, 36×57½ in. Jones Library, Amherst, MA.

the same footing as the Europeans.

The popularity of paintings of the Far West produced by Bierstadt, Whittredge, Kensett and Gifford encouraged a related group of painters who focused exclusively on western images and themes. The "Rocky Mountain School" has sometimes been labeled an extension of the Hudson River School, although the philosophy of its painters was not the same. Thomas Hill and Thomas Moran were major figures in the developing art world on the West Coast; their large, sometimes melodramatic paintings were exhibited in the East and often won prizes.

The spectacular 1876 Centennial Exposition in Philadelphia marked the beginning of the end of the Hudson River School. The Exposition's Memorial Hall contained in its thirty galleries the largest art exhibit ever displayed in the United States. Landscapes dominated the exhibit and won many of the medals, with Sanford Gifford winning the most awards. However, the most popular works at the Exposition were the paintings of a different landscape style, which were influenced by the revolutionary Barbizon style in France. These new, young artists painted directly on site – in the wind, mist or sun – and expressed on canvas their subjective emotional response to nature. Instead of rendering faithful detail, their scenes were more loosely painted and often more simplified.

Several of the Hudson River artists were intrigued rather than threatened with this new style and began to incorporate its elements into their own work. Whittredge and Alexander Wyant experimented with the new approach, but it was George Inness who allowed his art to be the most transformed by the Barbizon School. His later work in the Barbizon style is generally considered his best.

The young artists returning from Europe began to move into the Tenth Street studio building, hovering around William Merritt Chase, one of the new French-style painters.

Elaborately detailed studio paintings were frowned upon in favor of the more immediate freshness of the new style. Reflected in the journalism of the day, the conflict between the two styles continued at the National Academy of Design.

By the opening of the Metropolitan Museum of Art in 1880, an institution conceived and organized by William Cullen Bryant, John Kensett and others, the Hudson River painters had lost favor. The "Hudson River School" title was first created in the 1870s as a derogatory term comparing these earlier landscape painters to the newly fashionable French Barbizon painters.

Not until the 1940s did a full-scale resurrection of the Hudson River School of painting begin. In 1945, for the first time since the Centennial Exposition of 1876, an exhibition was organized to focus attention primarily on nineteenth-century landscapes. In 1987, the distinguished exhibit at the Metropolitan Museum of Art, "American Paradise: The World of the Hudson River School," reaffirmed the pivotal role of the landmark scenery painters in American art.

As the twentieth century finishes its course, many Americans have serious concerns about the remaining "wilderness" in the United States, including the health threat of increasing air and water pollution, and the loss of the natural landscape in urban areas. Americans increasingly recognize the fragility of the environment. For some, the preservation of the natural world is a spiritual issue as it was for Thomas Cole and Asher Durand; in an American society dominated by technology, the remaining landscape is again regarded as a repository of "high and holy meaning," and an "oasis." As the protection of the natural world from destruction is now of national concern, the reverence for nature embodied in early American landscape art reminds us of ideals relevant today. Thus, it is not surprising that in recent years we have seen a renewed respect toward the Hudson River School of painters.

Above left: Photograph of
Frederic E. Church, c. 1860.

Above right: Frederic Church,
sketch of the south facade of
his home, Olana, which the
artist designed; c. 1870, pencil,
ink, watercolor on paper,
13 × 21¹⁵⁄₁₆ in. Olana is located
in Hudson, NY.

Above: Thomas Moran, *The
Spirit of the Indian*, 1869, oil on
canvas, 32¼ × 48 in. Philbrook
Museum of Art, Tulsa, OK.

Right: An example of a work
by a French Barbizon
landscapist, Jean-Baptiste-
Camille Corot's *The Boatman of
Mortefontaine*, oil on canvas,
24 × 35⅜ in. The Frick
Collection, 1903, New York, NY.

THE FORMATIVE PHASE

Thomas Doughty, as the first self-acknowledged landscape painter in the United States, was an inspiration to several of the major Hudson River painters, notably Thomas Cole. Before his arrival in New York City in 1825, Cole was drawn to the small landscapes by Doughty exhibited at The Pennsylvania Academy of the Fine Arts. A hunter and fisherman, Doughty spent many enjoyable hours in the woods and countryside, and his love of the natural world was evident in his paintings. Doughty's *In the Catskills* (1836) and *Autumn on the Hudson* (1850) represent landscape motifs popular with the Hudson River artists, but these paintings lack the power, drama and deft painting style of the latter.

The Wetterhorn (1832) by Samuel F. B. Morse is an example of the tamed, idealized landscape paintings – often containing European themes – that preceded Thomas Cole. Morse was a multi-talented individual whose artistic achievements usually lie in the shadow of his mechanical inventions. He became an accomplished portrait painter but painted landscapes and grand salon works as well. Morse interrupted his painting to develop new technology such as the daguerrotype and telegraph; meanwhile, he remained a significant figure in the art world for many years as president of the National Academy of Design.

Asher Durand was originally a prominent engraver, and his attention to detail in his landscapes shows this influence. He became a portrait and genre painter as well, indicating his diversity of accomplishments. His *Kindred Spirits* (p.1) has stood for decades as the primary emblem of the Hudson River School. It combines two key ingredients: an ideal, untamed American scene, bathed in gentle light; and two of the major figures of the romantic landscape movement, William Cullen Bryant and Thomas Cole. The painting was presented as a gift to Bryant after Cole's death, a tribute to their special friendship and their equally important roles in the art world. Durand's other landscape works illustrate the classic approach of the Hudson River painters. Following Cole's death, Durand became the acknowledged leader of the landscape movement.

Thomas Cole's *The Oxbow* has been a favorite with museum audiences since its first appearance in 1836. This "View from Mt. Holyoke" was a popular vista also painted by Frederic Church and included in William Bartlett's *American Scenery* published in 1840. The painting combines a strong, elevated foreground with a stormy sky and "blasted tree" – evident in so many Hudson River School landscapes – with the serene and glorious valley stretched out below. The powerful design of the river oxbow completes the dynamic painting.

Cole's *The Voyage of Life* series of paintings represent the epitome of the idealized Romantic landscape combined with spiritual instruction and was a favorite of Cole's. The first set of "Voyage" paintings was commissioned by a wealthy patron for his private use; in wishing to exhibit the series as a highlight of his career, Cole immediately began a second set after finishing the first. Public exhibition of these paintings was poorly received, although a later series of engravings of the paintings became very popular. The second set of "Voyage" paintings ended up in obscurity on the walls of the Bethesda Home for the Aged in Cincinnati until 1962, when they were purchased by the National Gallery and given the prominence that Cole had originally intended.

THOMAS COLE

**View from Mount Holyoke, Northampton, Massachusetts,
after a Thunderstorm (The Oxbow), 1836**

Oil on canvas, 51½ × 76 in.
*The Metropolitan Museum of Art, New York, NY
Gift of Mrs. Russell Sage, 1908 (08.228)*

Thomas Cole

**The Voyage of Life:
Childhood,** 1842

Oil on canvas, 52⅞ × 77⅞ in.
*National Gallery of Art
Washington, D.C.
Ailsa Mellon Bruce Fund
(1971.16.1)*

THOMAS COLE
The Voyage of Life: Youth,
1842

Oil on canvas, 52⅞ × 76¾ in.
*National Gallery of Art
Washington, D.C.
Ailsa Mellon Bruce Fund
(1971.16.2)*

Thomas Cole
The Voyage of Life: Manhood,
1842

Oil on canvas, 52⅞ × 79¾ in.
National Gallery of Art
Washington, D.C.
Ailsa Mellon Bruce Fund
(1971.16.3)

THOMAS COLE
The Voyage of Life: Old Age,
1842

Oil on canvas, 52½ × 77¼ in.
National Gallery of Art
Washington, D.C.
Ailsa Mellon Bruce Fund
(1971.16.4)

THOMAS DOUGHTY (1793-1856)
In the Catskills, c. 1836
Oil on canvas, 30¼ × 42¼ in.
Addison Gallery of American Art
Phillips Academy, Andover, MA

Pages 36-37:

Thomas Doughty

Autumn on the Hudson, 1850

Oil on canvas, 34⅜ × 48½ in.
In the collection of The Corcoran Gallery of Art,
Washington, D.C. Gift of William Wilson Corcoran (69.70)

Asher B. Durand

River Scene, 1854

Oil on canvas, 24 × 34⅛ in.
© 1988 The Metropolitan Museum of Art, New York, NY
Bequest of Mary Starr Van Winkle, 1969 (1970.58)

ASHER B. DURAND

Interior of a Wood, c. 1850

Oil on canvas, 17×24 in.
Addison Gallery of American Art
Phillips Academy, Andover, MA
Gift of Mrs. Frederic Durand

Page 41:

SAMUEL F. B. MORSE (1791-1872)

The Wetterhorn and Falls of the Reichenbach, c. 1832

Oil on canvas, 23×16⅛ in.
© *The Newark Museum, Newark, NJ*
Bequest of Dr. J. Ackerman Coles, 1926 (26.1167)

Sᴀɴꜰᴏʀᴅ Rᴏʙɪɴꜱᴏɴ Gɪꜰꜰᴏʀᴅ (1823-1880)

Kauterskill Clove, 1862

Oil on canvas, 48 × 39⅞ in.
© 1987 The Metropolitan Museum of Art, New York, NY
Bequest of Maria DeWitt Jesup, 1914 (15.30.62)

The Mature Phase

The artists of the Hudson River School often camped, traveled and studied together, both in the United States and abroad. They shared with each other their favorite painting sites, motifs and points of view. A familiar Hudson River School format was a vertical composition of a densely wooded scene, sometimes with a brook, waterfall or pool serving as a point of focus. Asher Durand used this format in *Kindred Spirits*, and George Hetzel clearly based his *Rocky Gorge* on Durand's painting. *A Mountain Brook* by Arthur Parton documents the same approach.

For good reason, a major source of inspiration for artists of the Cole tradition was the Hudson River Valley; the dramatic mountain terrain ornamenting the valley offered contrast to the placid river, and constant changes in weather, season and time of day made the Hudson River Valley a dynamic and challenging subject. Jasper Cropsey's large (5 ft. × 9 ft.) canvas, *Autumn on the Hudson River*, so impressed Queen Victoria Cropsey achieved instant fame in England. Thereafter he proceeded to capitalize on his popular autumn scenes – which stood apart from other artwork – with his use of new, brighter pigments.

Samuel Colman's *Storm King on the Hudson* is an excellent example of highlighting special effects along the river, as shown by the heavy clouds gathered around the peak of Storm King Mountain. On the other hand, *The Hudson on the Tappan Zee* by Francis Silva, captures a tranquil scene near the mouth of the river. Silva was never prominent as a Hudson River artist, but recently his paintings have been seen as important Luminist works, specializing in lighting and atmosphere.

The Catskill Mountains were an important focus for many Hudson River painters. Accompanying Thomas Cole, the artists enjoyed many sketching parties in the mountains. Sanford Gifford's particular favorite spot was Kauterskill Clove, the subject of his painting, which is infused with a poetic, idealistic aura. The Catskill Mountain House, built in 1824, was the first of the grand tourist hotels that perched on sites with spectacular vistas. Jasper Cropsey and Sanford Gifford feature the mountain house from different vantage points in their paintings.

Further up the Hudson River Valley, the Adirondack Mountains began to draw summer sketching parties. It is interesting to compare William T. Richard's *A View of the Adirondacks* (1857) with Thomas Cole's *Schroon Mountain* (1838). Richards, a great admirer of Cole's, created a docile, pastoral landscape with strong but not threatening lighting contrasts. Cole's painting, on the other hand, is a typical "wilderness" painting, in which nature is untamed, mysterious and enticing.

The Lake George area of upstate New York is portrayed in various paintings by John Casilear, John Kensett and Martin Johnson Heade. Whereas Heade's interpretation minimized the spectacular and brought the different pieces of the environment into more equal scale, Kensett dramatized the mountain shoreline and emphasized tranquility and quality of light in the Luminist approach to painting. Kensett's *Lake George* (1869) is considered the finest of his many paintings of the subject.

Along with the Adirondacks, the mountains of New England drew many artists each summer, such as John Kensett, Aaron Shattuck and Sanford Gifford. Kensett and Shattuck paintings include favorite subjects of the region: Mt. Washington and Lake Chocorua. Kensett's *Mt. Washington* is a large painting, 40 in. x 60 in., while Shattuck's *Chocorua Lake and Mountain* is only 10 in. x 19 in., yet both works exemplify the same traditional Hudson River School treatment of their subject matter; the noble mountains predominate, rising from detailed and picturesque surroundings. In comparison, in his *The Wilderness*, Gifford rendered Mt. Katahdin of Maine somewhat differently; this painting includes the romantic Indian motif as a detail and is not only dominated by the majestic mountains but also by the idealistic light that softly imbues the entire canvas.

In the post-Civil War years, as the war-weary population returned to carefree summers and sojourns by the sea, paintings of the seashore, such as Worthington Whittredge's *Second Beach, Newport* (1878), became very popular. A number of artists shifted their attention from the mountains to the shore. Martin Johnson Heade painted seashore scenes from the start; his coastal storm paintings, such as *Storm Over Narragansett Bay* (1868), are powerful and intriguing. *Time and Tide* (1873) by Alfred Bricher is considered Bricher's best work, with its beauty of strength and simplicity. A latecomer to the Hudson River

School, Bricher changed from landscape to seascape painting in the early 1870s.

The wild and romantic subject matter of the western states suited the Hudson River School style as well. While journeying in the West in groups, landscape artists produced many paintings like Whittredge's *Crossing the Ford, Platte River*. Along with rendering landscapes of the East, these artists continued to create idealistic western scenes, often depicting the serenity of Indian life amidst nature.

As the growing group of Hudson River School painters wandered beyond the Northeast, any number of lovely or unique landscapes in the vast United States served as suitable subject matter. Both David Johnson and Frederic Church painted the fascinating landmark in Virginia known as Natural Bridge. Johnson's *Natural Bridge* was typical of how Hudson River School artists utilized an unusual natural formation to highlight the mystery and wonder of nature.

An accomplished portrait artist, Robert Duncanson used familiar picturesque locations in Ohio for his landscape work. A black citizen, Duncanson was educated in Scotland in the

1840s, with the benefit of funds from the Anti-Slavery League, and became one of the first internationally-known black American artists.

An architect as well as a painter, Jasper Cropsey found the recently-built Starucca Viaduct railroad in Pennsylvania an interesting subject to be included in a landscape. In Cropsey's idealized landscape, *Starruca Viaduct* (1865), the railroad is featured but does not intrude on the tranquil scene, in which nature is still supreme. As American industrialism and transportation network expanded, Cropsey's painting communicated the romantic view that technology would not necessarily damage the countryside if it remained only a minor intrusion on the enduring natural environment.

The Ruins of Caesar's Palace (1869) by Jervis McEntee reminds us how the Hudson River School painters were captivated by the romantic ruins of the Mediterranean region. Many of these painters would return from European travels to create paintings of actual or imaginary ruins. By the end of the 1870s, the subject matter of the Hudson River School painters had broadened to include the intriguing world beyond America.

Pages 44-45:

ALFRED THOMPSON BRICHER (1837-1908)

Time and Tide, c. 1873

Oil on canvas, 25¼ × 50 in.
Dallas Museum of Art
Foundation for the Art Collection
Gift of Mr. and Mrs. Frederick Mayer (1976.40)

JOHN WILLIAM CASILEAR (1811-1893)

Afternoon Near Lake George, 1856

Oil on canvas, 12 × 16 in.
Vassar College Art Gallery, Poughkeepsie, NY
Gift of Matthew Vassar (864.1.10)

SAMUEL COLMAN (1832-1920)

Storm King on the Hudson, 1866

Oil on canvas, 32⅛ × 59⅞ in.
National Museum of American Art
Smithsonian Institution, Washington, D.C.
Gift of John Gellatly (1929.6.20)

JASPER FRANCIS CROPSEY (1823-1900)
Catskill Mountain House, 1855

Oil on canvas, 29 × 44 in.
The Minneapolis Institute of Arts, MN
Bequest of Mrs. Lillian Lawhead Rinderer
in memory of her brother, William A. Lawhead,
and the William Hood Dunwoody Fund (32.47)

Pages 50-51:

Jasper F. Cropsey

Starrucca Viaduct, Pennsylvania, 1865

Oil on canvas, 22⅜ × 36⅜ in. *Toledo Museum of Art, Toledo, OH. Gift of Florence Scott Libbey, 1947 (47.58)*

Robert Scott Duncanson (c. 1821-1872)

Blue Hole, Little Miami River, 1851

Oil on canvas, 28½ × 41½ in. *Cincinnati Art Museum, Cincinnati, OH Gift of Norbert Heermann and Arthur Helbig (1926.18)*

SANFORD R. GIFFORD
The Wilderness, 1860

Oil on canvas, 30 × 54⁵⁄₁₆ in.
Toledo Museum of Art, Toledo, OH
Gift of Florence Scott Libbey, 1951 (51.403)

Sanford R. Gifford
Catskill Mountain House, 1862

Oil on canvas, 9⁵⁄₁₆ × 18½ in.
Austin Arts Center
Trinity College, Hartford, CT
George F. McMurray Collection

Martin Johnson Heade (1819-1904)

Lake George, 1862

Oil on canvas, 26 × 49¾ in.
Courtesy, Museum of Fine Arts, Boston
Bequest of Maxim Karolik (64.430)

Martin Johnson Heade

Lynn Meadows, 1863

Oil on canvas, 12 × 30⅛ in.
Yale University Art Gallery, New Haven, CT
Arnold H. Nichols, B.A., 1920 (1967.19)

Martin Johnson Heade

Approaching Storm: Beach Near Newport, c. 1860

Oil on canvas, 28 × 58¼ in.
Courtesy, Museum of Fine Arts, Boston, MA
M. and M. Karolik Collection (45.889)

Martin Johnson Heade

Thunderstorm Over Narragansett Bay, 1868

Oil on canvas, 32⅛ × 54½ in.
Amon Carter Museum, Fort Worth, TX

Page 65:
George Hetzel (1826-1899)

Rocky Gorge, 1869

Oil on canvas, 42 × 29 in.
Westmoreland Museum of Art, Greensburg, PA

David Johnson (1827-1908)
Natural Bridge, 1860
Oil on canvas, 14½ × 22¼ in.
*Reynolda House, Museum of American
Art, Winston-Salem, NC*

JOHN F. KENSETT
Lake George, 1869
Oil on canvas, 44⅛ × 66⅜ in.
© 1984 The Metropolitan
Museum of Art, New York, NY.
Bequest of Maria DeWitt Jesup,
1915 (15.30.61)

JERVIS MCENTEE (1828-1891)

The Ruins of Caesar's Palace, c. 1868

Oil on canvas, 24½ × 40⅛ in.
The Pennsylvania Academy of the Fine Arts
Purchased with funds from the Fine Arts Ball
and Discotheque. Courtesy of The Pennsylvania
Academy of the Fine Arts Women's Committee (1978.9)

Page 73:

ARTHUR PARTON (1842-1914)

A Mountain Brook, 1875

Oil on canvas, 52½ × 40½ in.
Museum of Fine Arts, Springfield, MA
Gift of Judge and Mrs. Ernest S. Fuller

WILLIAM TROST RICHARDS
(1833-1905)

A View in the Adirondacks,
c. 1857

*Oil on canvas, 30¼ × 44¼ in.
Henry Art Gallery, University
of Washington, Seattle, WA
Gift of J. W. Clise (58.4)*

AARON DRAPER SHATTUCK (1832-1928)

Chocorua Lake and Mountain, 1855

Oil on canvas, 10⅛ × 19⅝ in.
Vassar College Art Gallery, Poughkeepsie, NY
Gift of Matthew Vassar (864.1.64)

Francis Augustus Silva (1835-1886)
The Hudson at the Tappan Zee, 1876
Oil on canvas, 24⅟16 × 42³⁄16 in.
*The Brooklyn Museum, Brooklyn, NY
Dick S. Ramsey Fund (65.10)*

Page 78:

WORTHINGTON WHITTREDGE (1820-1910)

The Old Hunting Grounds, c. 1864

Oil on canvas, 36 × 27 in.
Reynolda House, Museum of American Art, Winston-Salem, NC

WORTHINGTON WHITTREDGE

Crossing the Ford, Platte River, Colorado, 1868 and 1870

Oil on canvas, 40¼ × 69⅛ in.
The Century Association, New York, NY

WORTHINGTON WHITTREDGE
The Camp Meeting, 1874
Oil on canvas, 16 × 40¹¹⁄₁₆ in.
© 1988 The Metropolitan Museum of Art
Amelia B. Lazarus Fund, 1913 (13.39.1)

Pages 82-83:

Worthington Whittredge

Second Beach, Newport, c. 1878-80

Oil on canvas, 30½ × 50¼ in.
Walker Art Center, Minneapolis, MN
Gift of the T. B. Walker Foundation

THE
EXPANSIONIST
PHASE

Young Frederic Church of Hartford, Connecticut, became a student of Thomas Cole's a few years before that great artist died. Dedicated to the representation of nature as Cole had been, Church was already exhibiting at the National Academy at the age of 19 and became a full member of the Academy at 23. Unlike Cole, however, Church did not struggle with conflicting ideals in his paintings; he had little interest in "moral instruction" and was committed only to accuracy of depiction.

Instead of pursuing the conventional path of European art training, Church's fascination with dramatic and exotic subjects repeatedly took him on lengthy journeys all over the world, often with fellow artists like Louis Mignot. While his early paintings, such as *Hooker and Company Journeying through the Wilderness* and *New England Scenery*, earned him respect, Church's dramatic new representation of Niagara Falls brought him fame. For this project, Church climbed a tree to get just the view of the falls that satisfied him and then executed an enormous monument of a painting; later, *Niagara* (1857) was the sole work to be featured in a New York gallery.

Following two trips to Ecuador, Church completed a series of stunning paintings based on his adventures. His meticulously detailed *The Heart of the Andes* exhibits Church's attention to scientific accuracy and was an artistic and popular sensation in his day. Contemporary news accounts reported "crowds of people who came to see the picture, and who could not find even standing room. . . . The exhibition was yielding nearly $600 a day!" In 1859, the painting sold for $10,000, contributing to Church's newfound affluence.

Unlike Church, Albert Bierstadt studied at length in Europe, spending time at the Dusseldorf Academy of Art, and in Rome with his companions Worthington Whittredge and Sanford Gifford. Soon after his return to the United States in 1858, Bierstadt painted the scenery of the Northeast. Within the next few years, as Bierstadt experienced exciting and dangerous trips to the remote Far West, these travels provided him with

material to produce his greatly successful grand-scale paintings. Although these paintings are comparable to Church's massive works in size, Bierstadt depicted the wilderness of the West with a subjective rather than scientific treatment.

His *Rocky Mountains – Landers Peak* was the main attraction at the Metropolitan Fair in 1864 and elevated Bierstadt to the pinnacle of Hudson River School success. In 1865, when the painting sold for $25,000, Bierstadt joined the ranks of wealthy landscape artists like Church. However, Bierstadt had only ten years of unchallenged glory during his heyday. The appearance of French Barbizon-influenced paintings at the 1876 Centennial Exposition in Philadelphia signaled the rapid descent of the Hudson River School.

A number of the Hudson River School artists were responsive to the new concepts from France, approaches to landscape painting that would be pushed even further by the Impressionists a few years later. The Barbizon paintings displayed more expressive brushwork, varieties of subject matter (including still lifes and interior scenes), and a subjective interpretation rather than faithful reproduction of detail.

Alexander Wyant and George Inness were just two of the Hudson River School painters who were able to survive the transition in popular taste and artistic development. The two were close friends and often painted together. Wyant's *Tennessee* (1866) and Inness's *Our Old Mill* (1849) reflect their strong early Hudson River styles, whereas *Clearing Up* (1869) and *Niagara Falls* (1885) by Inness are good examples of Barbizon-influenced work, demonstrating how, in Inness's words:

Details in the picture must be elaborated only fully enough to reproduce the impression that the artist wishes to reproduce. When more than this is done, the impression is weakened or lost, and we see simply an array of external things which may be very cleverly painted, and may look very real, but which do not make an artistic painting.

ALBERT BIERSTADT
Looking Up the Yosemite Valley, c. 1865-67
Oil on canvas, 36×58½ in.
Haggin Collection, The Haggin Museum, Stockton, CA

ALBERT BIERSTADT

A Storm in the Rocky Mountains – Mount Rosalie, 1866

Oil on canvas, 83 × 142¼ in.
The Brooklyn Museum, Brooklyn, NY
Dick S. Ramsay Fund, A. Augustus Healy Fund B,
Frank L. Babbott Fund, A. Augustus Healy Fund,
Ella C. Woodward Memorial Funds, Gift of Daniel M. Kelly,

Gift of Charles Simon, Charles Smith Memorial Fund,
Caroline Pratt Fund, Frederick Loeser Fund, Augustus
Graham School of Design Fund, Bequest of Mrs. William T. Brewster,
Gift of Mrs. W. Woodward Phelps, Gift of Seymour Barnard,
Charles Stuart Smith Fund, Bequest of Laura L.
Barnes, Gift of J. A. H. Bell, John B. Woodward
Memorial Fund, Bequest of Mark Finley (76.79)

ALBERT BIERSTADT

Donner Lake at the Summit, 1873

Oil on canvas, 72×120 in.
Courtesy of The New-York Historical Society, New York, NY

ALBERT BIERSTADT

**The Morteratsch Glacier, Upper Engadine Valley,
Pontresina,** 1895

Oil on canvas, 72×120 in.
*The Brooklyn Museum, Brooklyn, NY
Gift of Mrs. Mary Stewart Bierstadt (03.69)*

Frederic Edwin Church (1826-1900)

**Hooker and Company Journeying through the
Wilderness from Plymouth to Hartford in 1636,** 1846

Oil on canvas, 40¼ × 60³⁄₁₆ in.
Wadsworth Atheneum, Hartford, CT

FREDERIC E. CHURCH

New England Scenery, 1851

Oil on canvas, 36×53 in.
George Walter Vincent Smith Art Museum,
Springfield, MA (1.23.24)

FREDERIC E. CHURCH
Niagara, 1857
Oil on canvas 42¼ × 90½ in.
In the collection of The Corcoran Gallery of Art,
Washington, D.C. Museum Purchase, Gallery Fund

FREDERIC E. CHURCH

Heart of the Andes, 1859

Oil on canvas, 66⅛ × 119¼ in.
© 1979/80 *The Metropolitan Museum of Art, New York, NY*
Bequest of Margaret E. Dows, 1909 (09.95)

FREDERIC E. CHURCH

Cotopaxi, 1862

Oil on canvas, 48×85 in.
© *The Detroit Institute of Arts, Detroit, MI. Founders Society*
Purchase, with funds from Mr. and Mrs. Richard A. Manoogian,
Robert H. Tannahill Foundation Fund, Gibbs Williams Fund,
Dexter M. Ferry, Jr., Fund, Merrill Fund, and Beatrice W. Rogers Fund (76.89)

Frederic E. Church
The Parthenon, 1871

Oil on canvas, 44½ × 72⅝ in.
© 1986 The Metropolitan Museum of Art, New York, NY
Bequest of Maria DeWitt Jesup, from the collection
of her husband, Morris K. Jesup, 1914 (15.30.67)

George Inness (1825-1894)

Our Old Mill, 1849

Oil on canvas, 30×42 in.
© 1988 The Art Institute of Chicago, All Rights Reserved
The Goodman Fund (1939.388)

George Inness (1825-1894)

Clearing Up, 1860

Oil on canvas, 15¼ × 25¾ in.
George Walter Vincent Smith Art Museum,
Springfield, MA (1.23.38)

GEORGE INNESS

Niagara Falls, 1885

Oil on wood, 15⅞ × 24 in.
National Museum of American Art
Smithsonian Institution, Washington, D.C.
Gift of John Gellatly (1929.6.67)

Louis Rémy Mignot (1831-1870)

Lagoon of the Guayaquil River, Ecuador, 1863

Oil on canvas, 24¼ × 38 in.
© *The Detroit Institute of Arts, Detroit, MI*
Founders Society Purchase, Beatrice W. Rogers
Bequest Fund and contributions from Robert H.
Tannahill and Al (Abraham) Borman (68.345)

Alexander Helwig Wyant (1836-1892)

Tennessee, 1866

Oil on canvas, 34¾ × 53¾ in.
© 1984 The Metropolitan Museum of Art, New York, NY. Gift of Mrs. George E. Schanck,
in memory of her brother, Arthur Hoppock Hearn, 1913 (13.53)

LIST OF COLOR PLATES

Picture Credits
All pictures were provided by the credited institution, except those supplied by the following:
Jones Library, Inc., Amherst, MA: page 18(right)
Library of Congress, Washington, D.C.: page 7(bottom)
Munson-Williams-Proctor Institute, Utica, NY: page 7(top)
Museum of Fine Arts, Boston, M. and M. Karolik Collection: page 9
National Portrait Gallery, Smithsonian Institution, Washington, D.C.: page 18(left)

The New York Public Library, New York, NY: pages 6(all), 14(middle, bottom)
New York State Office of Parks, Recreation and Historic Preservation, Olana State Historic Site: page 19(top, both)

Acknowledgments
The author and publisher would like to thank Janet Wu York, who edited and picture researched this book; and Sue Rose, who designed it.